Hot Math Topics

Problem Solving, Communication, and Reasoning

# Multiplication and Division

grade 4

Carole Greenes
Linda Schulman Dacey
Rika Spungin

Dale Seymour Publications®
Parsippany, New Jersey

This book is published by

**Dale Seymour Publications**
An imprint of Pearson Learning
299 Jefferson Road, P.O. Box 480
Parsippany, NJ 07054-0480

*www.pearsonlearning.com*

1-800-321-3106

Managing Editor: Catherine Anderson
Senior Editor: John Nelson
Project Editor: Mali Apple
Production/Manufacturing Director: Janet Yearian
Sr. Production/Manufacturing Coordinator: Fiona Santoianni
Design Director: Phyllis Aycock
Cover and Interior Illustrations: Jared Lee
Text and Cover Design: Tracey Munz
Composition and Computer Graphics: Alan Noyes

ISBN 0-7690-0003-7

2 3 4 5 6 7 8 9 10-ML-03 02 01

# Contents

# Introduction

## Why Was *Hot Math Topics* Developed?

The *Hot Math Topics* series was developed for several reasons:

- to offer students practice and maintenance of previously learned skills and concepts
- to enhance problem solving and mathematical reasoning abilities
- to build literacy skills
- to nurture collaborative learning behaviors

### Practicing and maintaining concepts and skills

Although textbooks and core curriculum materials do treat the topics explored in this series, their treatment is often limited by the lesson format and the page size. As a consequence, there are often not enough opportunities for students to practice newly acquired concepts and skills related to the topics, or to connect the topics to other content areas. *Hot Math Topics* provides the necessary practice and mathematical connections.

Similarly, core instructional programs often do not do a very good job of helping students maintain their skills. Although textbooks do include reviews of previously learned material, they are frequently limited to sidebars or boxed-off areas on one or two pages in each chapter, with four or five exercises in each box. Each set of problems is intended only as a sampling of previously taught topics, rather than as a complete review. In the selection and placement of the review exercises, little or no attention is given to levels of complexity of the problems. By contrast, *Hot Math Topics* targets specific topics and gives students more experience with concepts and skills related to them. The problems are sequenced by difficulty, allowing students to hone their skills. And, because they are not tied to specific lessons, the problems can be used at any time.

### Enhancing problem solving and mathematical reasoning abilities

*Hot Math Topics* present students with situations in which they may use a variety of problem solving strategies, including

- designing and conducting experiments to generate or collect data
- guessing, checking, and revising guesses
- organizing data in lists or tables in order to identify patterns and relationships
- choosing appropriate computational algorithms and deciding on a sequence of computations
- using inverse operations in "work backward" solution paths

For their solutions, students are also required to bring to bear various methods of reasoning, including

- deductive reasoning
- inductive reasoning
- proportional reasoning

For example, to solve clue-type problems, students must reason deductively and make inferences about mathematical relationships in order to generate candidates for the solutions and to home in on those that meet all of the problem's conditions.

To identify and continue a pattern and then write a rule for finding the next term in that pattern, students must reason inductively.

To compute unit prices and convert measurement units, students must reason proportionally.

To estimate or compare magnitudes of numbers, or to determine the type of number appropriate for a given situation, students must apply their number sense skills.

### Building communication and literacy skills

*Hot Math Topics* offers students opportunities to write and talk about mathematical ideas. For many problems, students must describe their solution paths, justify their solutions, give their opinions, or write or tell stories.

Some problems have multiple solution methods. With these problems, students may have to compare their methods with those of their peers and talk about how their approaches are alike and different.

Other problems have multiple solutions, requiring students to confer to be sure they have found all possible answers.

### Nurturing collaborative learning behaviors

Several of the problems can be solved by students working together. Some are designed specifically as partner problems. By working collaboratively, students can develop expertise in posing questions that call for clarification or verification, brainstorming solution strategies, and following another person's line of reasoning.

## What Is in *Multiplication and Division*?

This book contains 100 problems and tasks that focus on multiplication and division of whole numbers. Some problems involve addition and subtraction as well. The mathematics content, the mathematical connections, the problem solving strategies, and the communication skills that are emphasized are described below.

### Mathematics content

The multiplication and division problems and tasks require students to

- multiply and divide—basic facts
- multiply two-, three-, and four-digit numbers by single-digit numbers
- divide two-, three-, and four-digit numbers by single-digit numbers
- multiple and divide by multiples of 10
- compute with money
- estimate products and quotients involving greater numbers
- interpret remainders
- use alternative computational strategies

### Mathematical connections

In these problems and tasks, connections are made to these other topic areas:

- algebra
- geometry
- graphs
- measurement
- number theory

### Problem solving strategies

*Multiplication and Division* problems and tasks offer students opportunities to use one or more of several problem solving strategies.

- **Formulate Questions:** When data are presented in displays or text form, students must pose one or more questions that can be answered using the given data.
- **Complete Stories:** When confronted with an incomplete story, students must supply the missing information and then check that the story makes sense.
- **Organize Information:** To ensure that all possible solution candidates for a problem are considered, students may have to organize information using a picture, list, diagram, or table.
- **Guess, Check, and Revise:** In some problems, students have to identify candidates for the solution and then check whether those candidates match the conditions of the problem. If the conditions are not satisfied, other possible solutions must be generated and verified.
- **Identify and Continue Patterns:** To identify the next term or terms in a sequence, students have to recognize the relationship between successive terms and then generalize that relationship.
- **Use Logic:** Students have to reason deductively, from clues, to make inferences about the solution to a problem. They must reason proportionately to determine which of two buys is better. They have to reason inductively to continue numeric patterns.
- **Work backward:** In some problems, the output is given and students must determine the input by identifying mathematical relationships between the input and output and applying inverse operations.

### Communication skills

Problems and tasks in *Multiplication and Division* are designed to stimulate communication. As part of the solution process, students may have to

- describe their thinking steps
- describe patterns and rules
- find alternate solution methods and solution paths
- identify other possible answers
- formulate problems for classmates to solve
- compare solutions and methods with classmates

These communication skills are enhanced when students interact with one another and with the teacher. By communicating both orally and in writing, students develop their understanding and use of the language of mathematics.

## How Can *Hot Math Topics* Be Used?

The problems may be used as practice of newly learned concepts and skills, as maintenance of previously learned ideas, and as enrichment experiences for early finishers or more advanced students.

They may be used in class or assigned for homework. If used during class, they may be selected to complement lessons dealing with a specific topic or assigned every week as a means of keeping skills alive and well.

Because the problems often require the application of various problem solving strategies and reasoning methods, they may also form the basis of whole-class lessons whose goals are to develop expertise with specific problem solving strategies or methods.

The problems, which are sequenced from least to most difficult, may be used by students working in pairs or on their own. The selection of problems may be made by the teacher or the students based on their needs or interests. If the plan is for students to choose problems, you may wish to copy individual problems onto card stock and laminate them, and establish a problem card file.

To facilitate record keeping, a Management Chart is provided on page 6. The chart can be duplicated so that there is one for each student. As a problem is completed, the space corresponding to that problem's number may be shaded. An Award Certificate is included on page 6 as well.

## How Can Student Performance Be Assessed?

*Multiplication and Division* problems and tasks provide you with opportunities to assess students'

- knowledge of multiplication and division of whole numbers
- problem solving abilities
- mathematical reasoning methods
- communication skills

### Observations

Keeping anecdotal records helps you to remember important information you gain as you observe students at work. To make observations more manageable, limit each observation to a group of from four to six students or to one of the areas noted above. You may find that using index cards facilitates the recording process.

### Discussions

Many of the *Multiplication and Division* problems and tasks allow for multiple answers or may be solved in a variety of ways. This built-in richness motivates students to discuss their work with one another. Small groups or class discussions are appropriate. As students share their approaches to the problems, you will gain additional insights into their content knowledge, mathematical reasoning, and communication abilities.

### Scoring responses

You may wish to holistically score students' responses to the problems and tasks. The simple scoring rubric below uses three levels: high, medium, and low.

| High | Medium | Low |
|---|---|---|
| • Solution demonstrates that the student knows the concepts and skills.<br>• Solution is complete and thorough.<br>• Student communicates effectively. | • Solution demonstrates that the student has some knowledge of the concepts and skills.<br>• Solution is complete.<br>• Student communicates somewhat clearly. | • Solution shows that the student has little or no grasp of the concepts and skills.<br>• Solution is incomplete or contains major errors.<br>• Student does not communicate effectively. |

### Portfolios

Having students store their responses to the problems in *Hot Math Topics* portfolios allows them to see improvement in their work over time. You may want to have them choose examples of their best responses for inclusion in their permanent portfolios, accompanied by explanations as to why each was chosen.

### Students and the assessment process

Involving students in the assessment process is central to the development of their abilities to reflect on their own work, to understand the assessment standards to which they are held accountable, and to take ownership for their own learning. Young children may find the reflective process difficult, but with your coaching, they can develop such skills.

Discussion may be needed to help students better understand your standards for performance. Ask students such questions as, "What does it mean to communicate *clearly*?" "What is a *complete* response?" Some students may want to use a rubric to score their responses.

Participation in peer-assessment tasks will also help students to better understand the performance standards. In pairs or small groups, students can review each other's responses and offer feedback. Opportunities to revise work may then be given.

## What Additional Materials Are Needed?

Although manipulative materials and measurement devices are not required for solving the problems, if they are available in the classroom, they may be useful for some students. For *Multiplication and Division,* decimal models such as base ten blocks and decimal squares may be helpful. Chips, tiles or squares of paper, grid paper, one-inch cubes, and play money also may be useful. For drawing purposes, colored pencils, markers, and rulers should be readily accessible. Calculators are suggested for use with some of the problems and may be helpful to students in solving other problems as well.

## Management Chart

Name ______________________________

When a problem or task is completed, shade the box with that number.

| 1 | 2 | 3 | 4 | 5 | 6 | 7 | 8 | 9 | 10 |
|---|---|---|---|---|---|---|---|---|---|
| 11 | 12 | 13 | 14 | 15 | 16 | 17 | 18 | 19 | 20 |
| 21 | 22 | 23 | 24 | 25 | 26 | 27 | 28 | 29 | 30 |
| 31 | 32 | 33 | 34 | 35 | 36 | 37 | 38 | 39 | 40 |
| 41 | 42 | 43 | 44 | 45 | 46 | 47 | 48 | 49 | 50 |
| 51 | 52 | 53 | 54 | 55 | 56 | 57 | 58 | 59 | 60 |
| 61 | 62 | 63 | 64 | 65 | 66 | 67 | 68 | 69 | 70 |
| 71 | 72 | 73 | 74 | 75 | 76 | 77 | 78 | 79 | 80 |
| 81 | 82 | 83 | 84 | 85 | 86 | 87 | 88 | 89 | 90 |
| 91 | 92 | 93 | 94 | 95 | 96 | 97 | 98 | 99 | 100 |



## Award Certificate

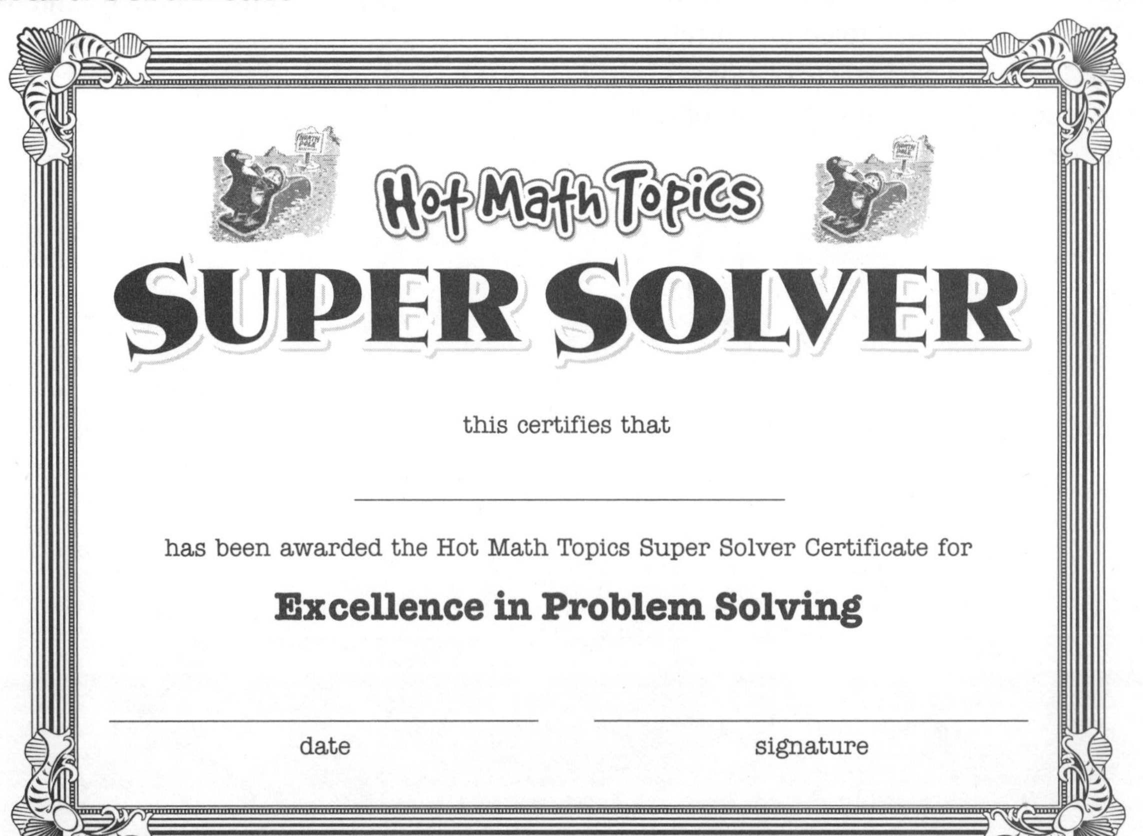

# Problems and Tasks

**Solve each number mystery.**
**Use the numbers given.**

**Mystery 1**

When you multiply the numbers, you get 24.

When you divide the numbers, you get 6.

The numbers are ______ and ______ .

**Mystery 2**

When you multiply the numbers, you get 36.

When you divide the numbers, you get 4.

The numbers are ______ and ______ .

**Write two number mysteries of your own.**



---

**Clues**

- I am greater than $5 \times 10$.
- I am less than $7 \times 9$.
- My tens digit is 5 more than my ones digit.

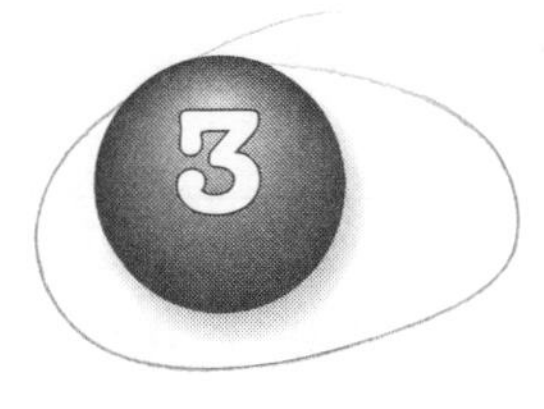


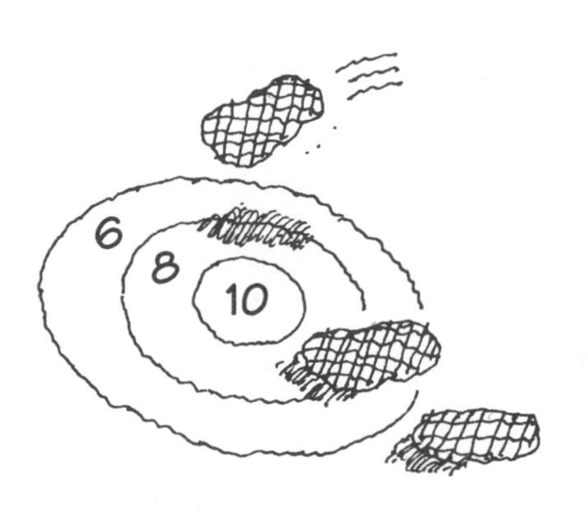

**Alana and Dan took turns.**

**They each threw 3 beanbags that all landed on the target.**

**Alana got the highest possible total score.**

**Dan got the lowest possible total score.**

**How many more points did Alana get than Dan?**

---

**4**

**purple**

**huge**

**7**

**3**

**21**

**clowns**

**lollipops**

**Write a math story problem.**

**Use the words and numbers shown here in your story.**

©Addison Wesley Longman, Inc./Published by Dale Seymour Publications®

How much more money is there in dimes than in quarters?

---

**Each ball weighs the same amount.**

**The can weighs the same as two balls.**

**How much does the can weigh?**

**Explain how you know.**

7

**Imagine that you have 40 tickets.**

**Which rides would you choose?**

**How many times would you go on each ride?**

**Would you have any tickets left over?**

---

8

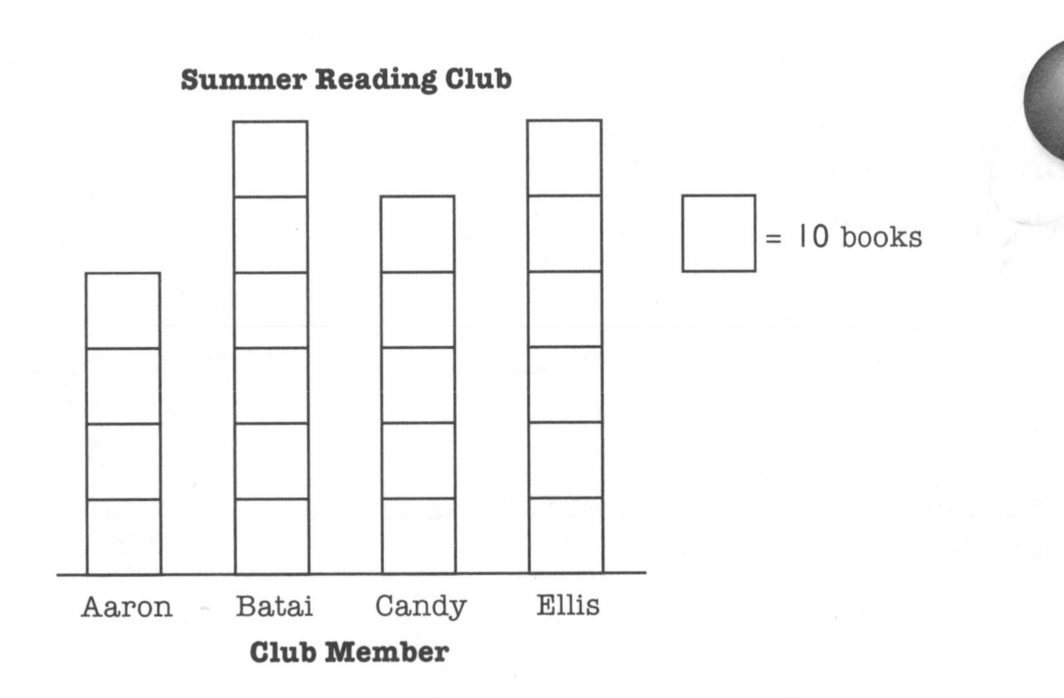


**How many more books did Batai read than Aaron?**

**Tell two ways to decide.**

9

**You want 24 tickets.**

**How many tickets should you pay for?**

**How many tickets will you get free?**

---

10

**Find the number.**

9 18 22 28 7

**Clues**

- It is less than $5 \times 5$.
- It is greater than $28 \div 4$.
- When you divide it by 4, the remainder is 2.
- It is a multiple of 3.

**Write clues for finding another one of the numbers.**

**Trade clues with a classmate.**

11

**Jackie wants to buy her sister 20 roses for her twentieth birthday.**

**How much will they cost?**

12

**The Lopez family went to the matinee.**

**They paid $16 for their tickets.**

**The total cost of the children's tickets was the same as the total cost of the adults' tickets.**

**How many children went to the movie?**

## 13

**Fill in each blank with a number.**

**The story must make sense.**

Jen bought _____ shirts for $_____ each.

She bought _____ pairs of socks for $_____ each.

Altogether she spent $_____ for shirts and socks.

---

## 14

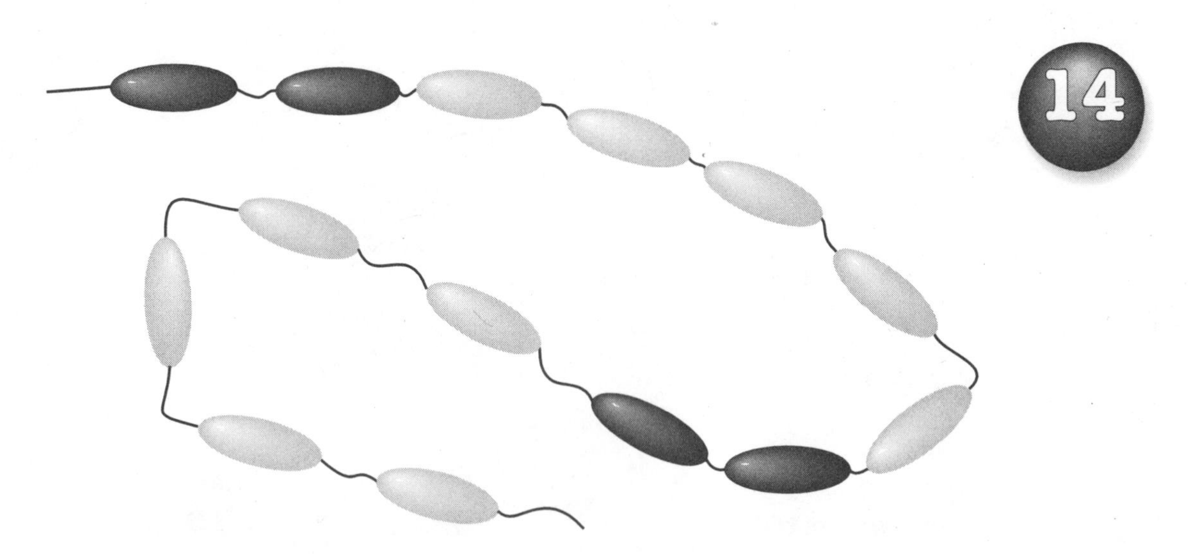

**The pattern continues.**

**There are 63 beads in the string.**

**How many beads are there?**

**How many beads are there?**



©Addison Wesley Longman, Inc./Published by Dale Seymour Publications®

15

**There are 16 students in the art studio.**

**The number of boys divided by the number of girls is 3.**

**How many boys are in the art studio?**

---

16

**Get 36 square tiles, or use grid paper.**

**Make a rectangle.**

**How many *different* rectangles can you make?**

**Record the length and width of each rectangle.**

17

How many  will you need to balance 18 ?

Tell how you decided.



18

Yvonne's class is taking a field trip to the beach.

There are 26 children in the class.

Each parent volunteer can drive up to 4 children.

All cars will leave at the same time.

How many parent volunteers are needed?

**Jeff has more than 4 coins.**

**When he puts his coins in stacks of 3, he has 1 coin left over.**

**When he puts his coins in stacks of 4, he has no coins left over.**

**What is the fewest number of coins Jeff could have?**

**Explain how you know.**

---

**Jonah has nickels and dimes.**

**He has 9 coins in all.**

**The value of the coins is 70¢.**

**How many dimes does Jonah have?**

**Count by 3s to 50. Put an X on the numbers you say.**

**Count by 4s to 50. Color the numbers red.**

| 1 | 2 | 3 | 4 | 5 | 6 | 7 | 8 | 9 | 10 |
|---|---|---|---|---|---|---|---|---|---|
| 11 | 12 | 13 | 14 | 15 | 16 | 17 | 18 | 19 | 20 |
| 21 | 22 | 23 | 24 | 25 | 26 | 27 | 28 | 29 | 30 |
| 31 | 32 | 33 | 34 | 35 | 36 | 37 | 38 | 39 | 40 |
| 41 | 42 | 43 | 44 | 45 | 46 | 47 | 48 | 49 | 50 |

**Which numbers are red and have an X?**

**What's the next number after 50 that would be red and have an X? How do you know?**



---

**Sanford spent 30¢ on stamps.**

**What stamps did he buy?**

**Make a list to show all the ways Sanford could have spent 30¢.**

Ben is 6 years older than Joel.

Joel is 3 times as old as Kai.

Kai is 14 years old.

How old is Ben?

Keenan is 2 years younger than Joy.

Joy is 4 times as old as Manuel.

Manuel is celebrating his first birthday.

How old is Keenan?

---

Find the number of kilograms on scale C.

Explain your thinking.

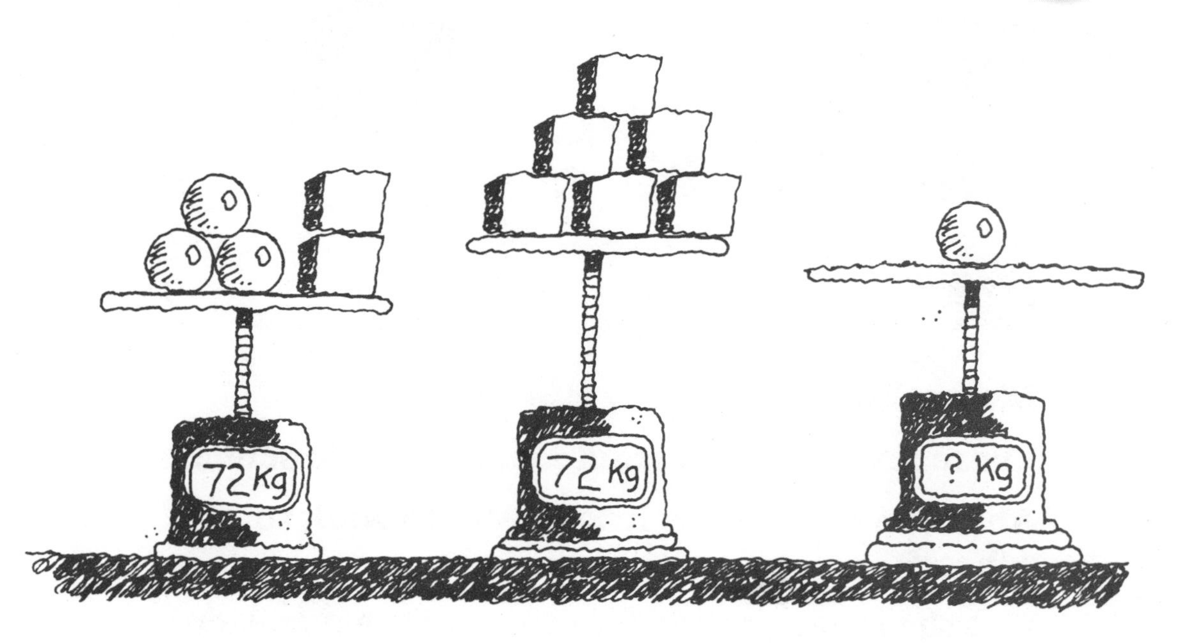

25

**Use the facts.**

**Write a question for each answer on the Answer Sign.**

**Facts**

- Daniela has 6 nickels and 5 pennies.
- Paul has 10 nickels and 3 pennies.



---

26

**Mei walks 3 blocks in 6 minutes.**

**There are 17 blocks from Mei's home to school.**

**About how long does it take Mei to walk to school?**

**List the steps you used to answer the question.**

27

The shop has 3 kinds of bread and 2 kinds of filling.

You can choose one of each.

How many different sandwiches can you make?
Make a list.

Suppose there are 4 kinds of bread and 5 fillings.

How many different sandwiches could you make?
How did you decide?

---

28

At least one of the coins in the bag is a dime.

What are the coins in the bag?



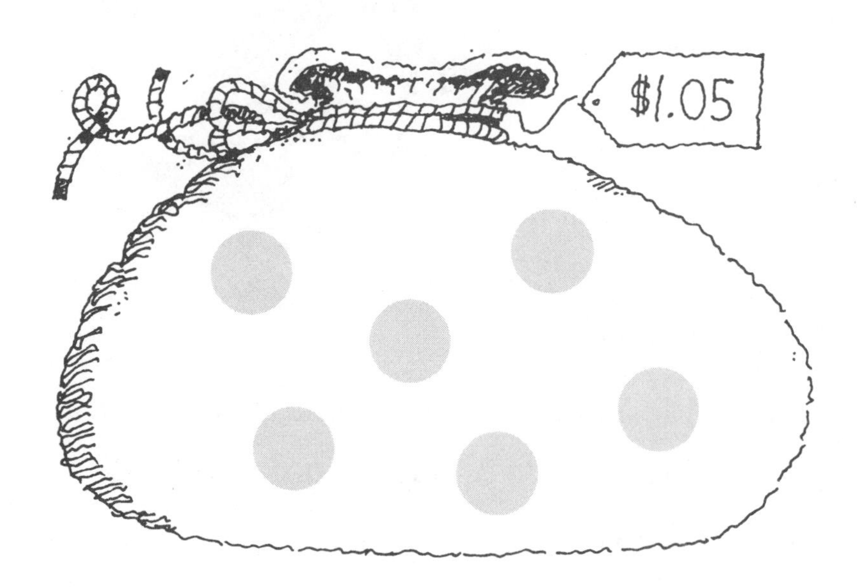

**Choose two of these numbers.**

**Find their product.**

# 12 4 8 2 6

**How many different products can you make?**

**Make a list.**



---

30

**Clues**

- When you divide me by 2, the remainder is 0.
- When you divide me by 3, the remainder is 0.
- I am between 40 and 45.

31

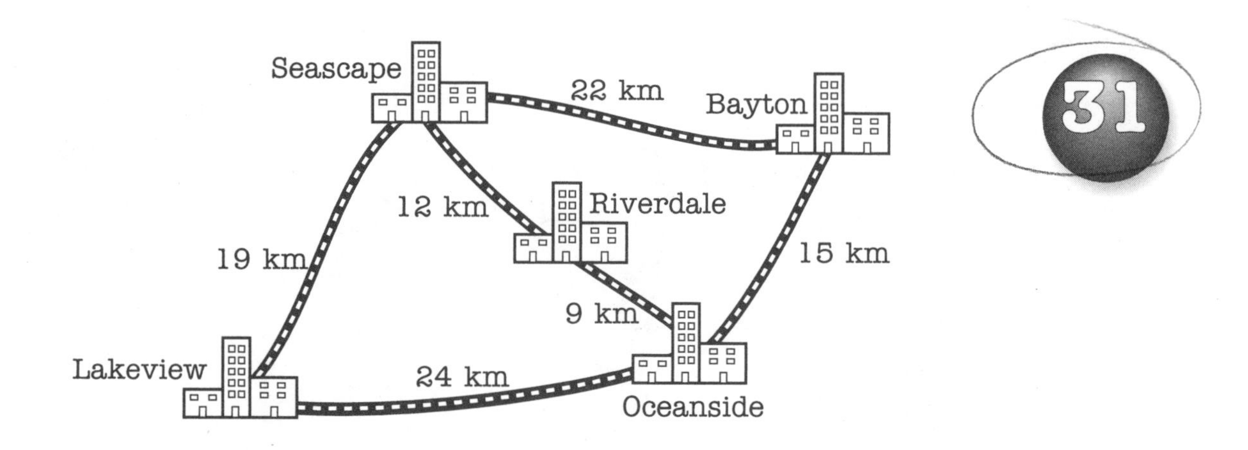


**Ms. Mindez drives to work every day, Monday through Friday.**

**Her home is in Lakeview. Her office is in Riverdale.**

**She takes the shortest route.**

**How many kilometers does Ms. Mindez drive back and forth to work each week?**

---

32

**Which offer is the better buy?**

**Tell how you know.**

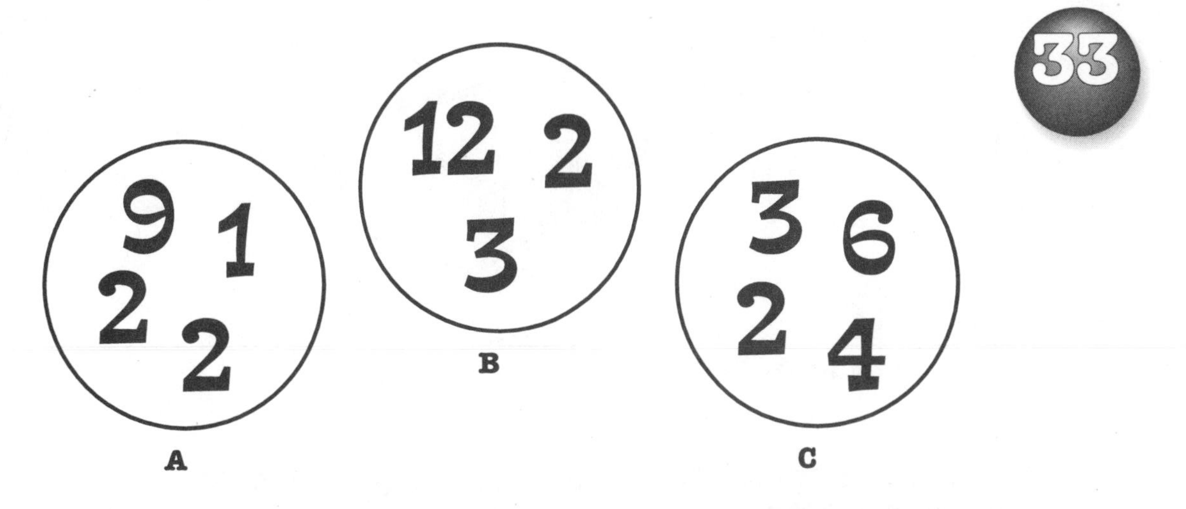


**Move one number from one circle to another.**

**Make the product of the numbers in each circle 72.**

**What did you move?**

---

**Write a number in each square to complete the loop.**

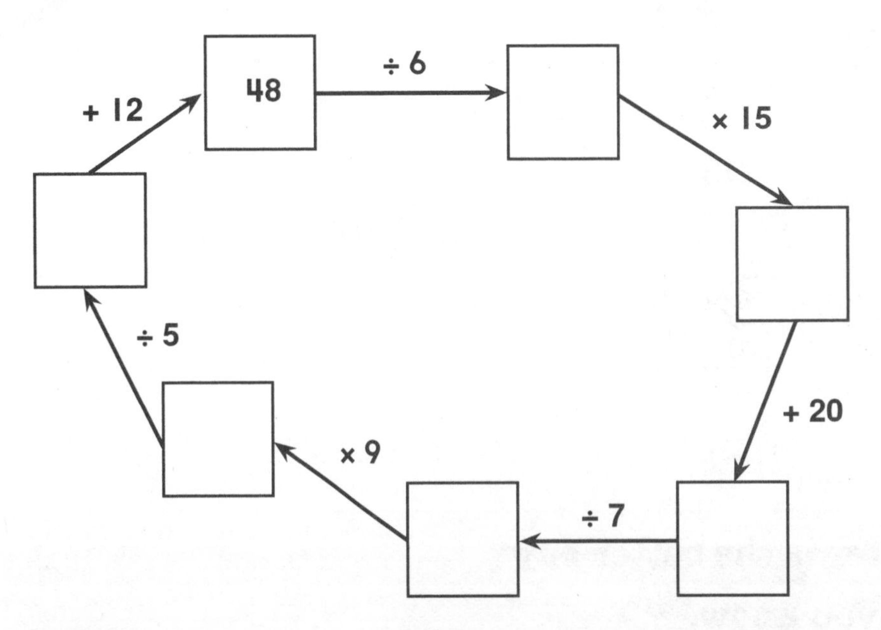


**Make up your own number loop with at least 2 multiplication and 2 division problems.**



©Addison Wesley Longman, Inc./Published by Dale Seymour Publications®

35

**There are 3 more basketball teams than baseball teams.**

**There are 5 teams altogether.**

**How many players are there in all?**

**Explain.**

---

**Find all the numbers you can for □ and △ that make the equation true.**

$$(\square \div 2) + \triangle = 10$$

**Make a table to show the numbers.**

| □ | |
|---|---|
| △ | |

Arrange the digits 3, 4, and 5
to make the greatest product.

Now arrange 7, 8, and 9 to make the greatest product.

When you want to make the greatest product, where should you place the greatest digit? The least digit? The middle digit?

Lelia made silk flowers just like this one.

She made 72 leaves.

How many petals did she make?

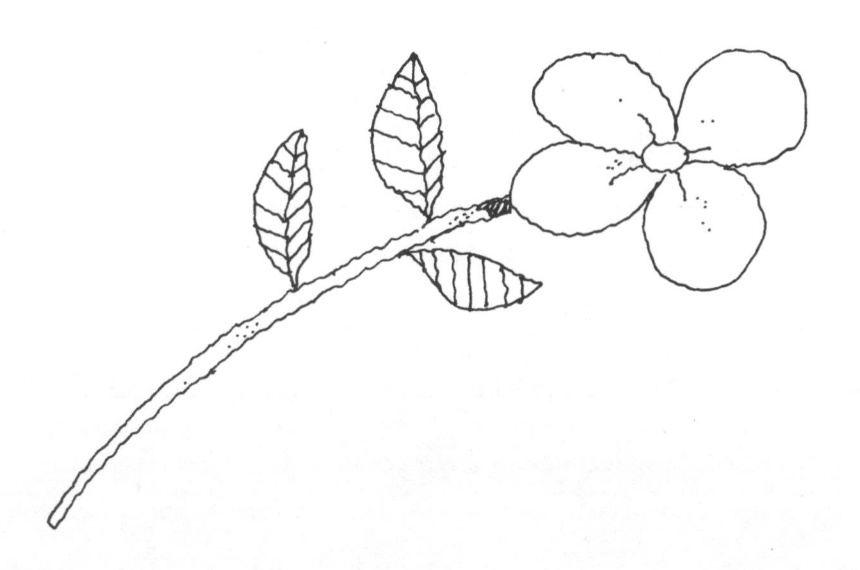

## 39

**Fill in the blanks with numbers.**

**The story must make sense.**

On the school bus there are _____ rows of seats.

There are _____ seats in each row.

Today there are _____ children on the bus.

There are _____ empty seats.

---



## 40

**You have a coupon for 24 free valentines.**

**What kind will you choose?**

**Why?**

**If you had to pay for the valentines, how much would they cost?**

**Use the numbers 3, 4, and 6.**

**Put one number in each box to make the smallest quotient.**

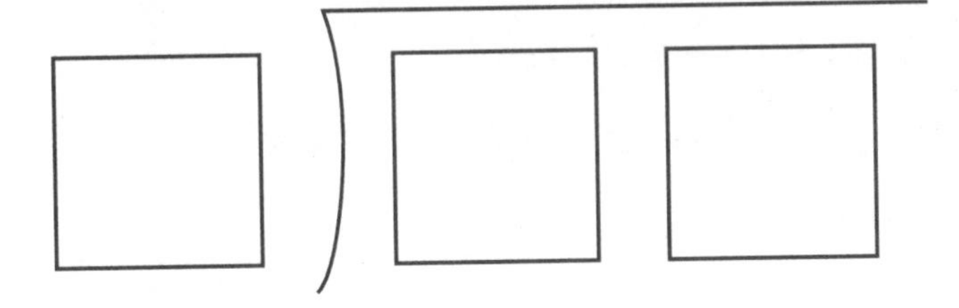

**What's your choice?**

**Tell why.**

or

**a nickel a day for each day in July**

**a quarter a day for 2 weeks**

**Each block costs $3.**

**How much does the structure cost?**

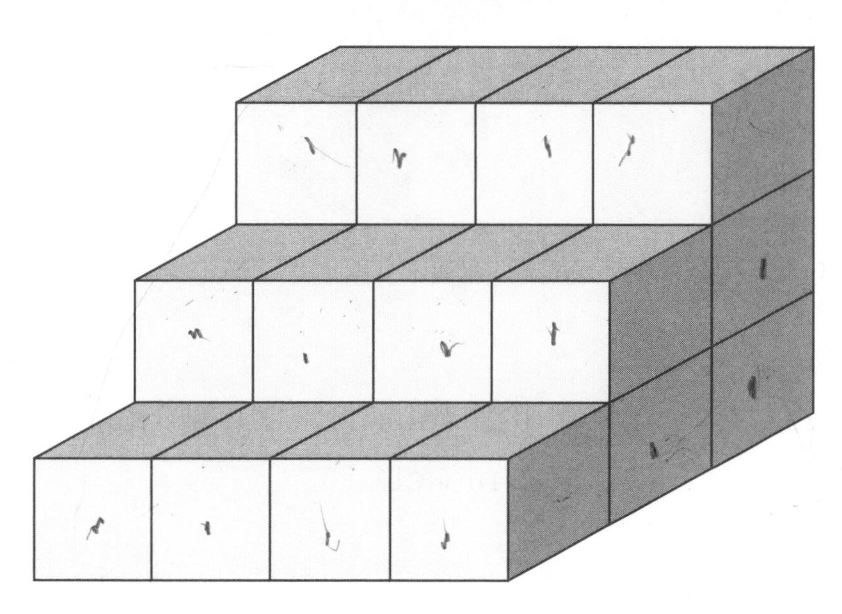

**Draw or build a structure that costs $60.**

---

 ×  × 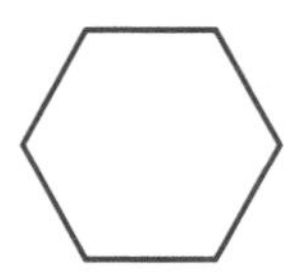 = 60

△ × 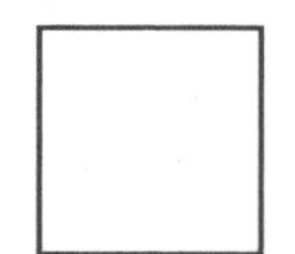 = 20

 ×  = 12

 = ?  = ? 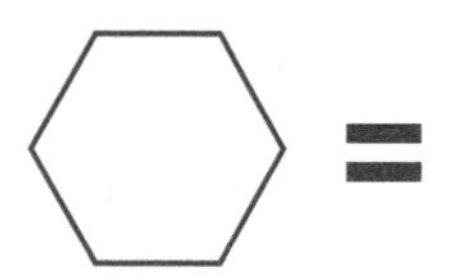 = ?


©Addison Wesley Longman, Inc./Published by Dale Seymour Publications®

**Clues**

- I have dimes, nickels, and pennies.
- I have 4 more dimes than nickels.
- I have 2 pennies.
- I have less than $1.
- I have more than 80¢.



---

**Mari has 52 stickers.**

**Abdul has 4 times as many stickers as Mari.**

**Chad has half as many stickers as Abdul.**

**How many stickers do they have in all?**

**Ang had to multiply 3 × 45.**

**He wrote:**

| | |
|---|---|
| **Step 1:** | $3 \times 50 = 150$ |
| **Step 2:** | $3 \times 5 = 15$ |
| **Step 3:** | $150 - 15 = 135$ |
| **Step 4:** | $3 \times 45 = 135$ |

**Multiply 4 × 29 using Ang's method.**

**Show the steps.**

---

48

**Finish the story.**

**Put one number from the shells on each line.**

**Be sure the story makes sense.**

Jackie had ______ shells.

He put ______ shells in each box and had ______ shells left over.

He gave ______ boxes, or ______ shells, to his sister, Jan.

**What does the puzzle cost?**

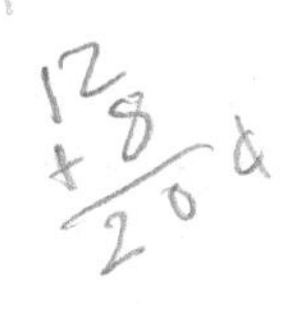

49

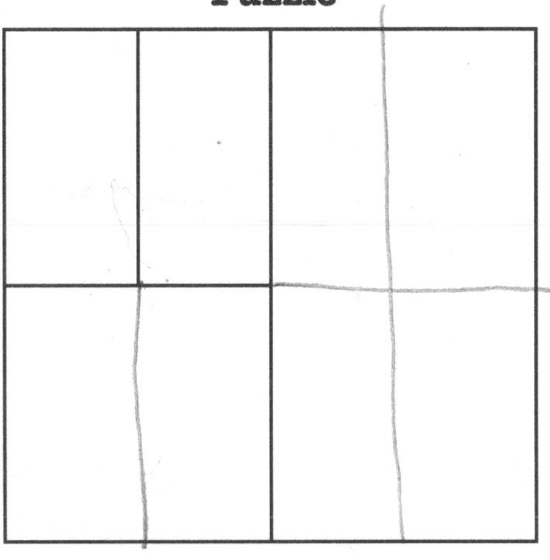


= 12¢



**What is the first number in row 10?**

50

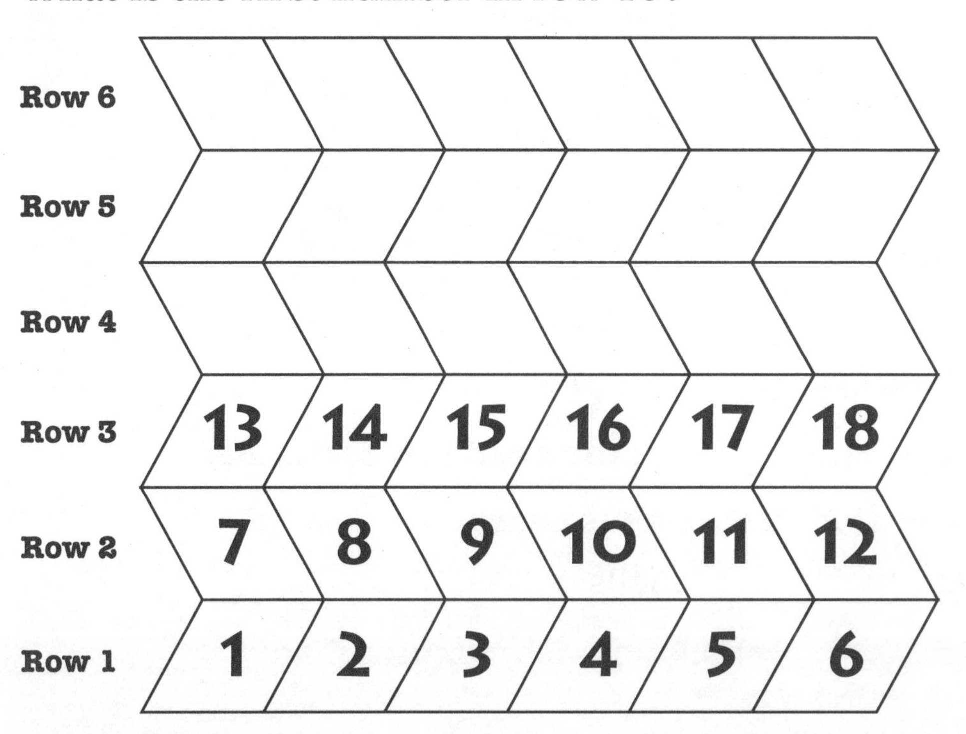


**Tell how you know.**

## 51

**300 183 250**

**213 270**

**Which of these is the mystery number?**

**The mystery number is**

- less than $7 \times 41$.
- greater than $6 \times 34$.
- a multiple of 3.
- not $27 \times 10$.

**What is the mystery number?**

---

## 52

**The Science Club sold cookies to raise money for a telescope.**

**The police department bought half of all the chocolate chip cookies.**

**How many cookies did the police buy?**

**Science Club Cookie Sale**

Chocolate chip 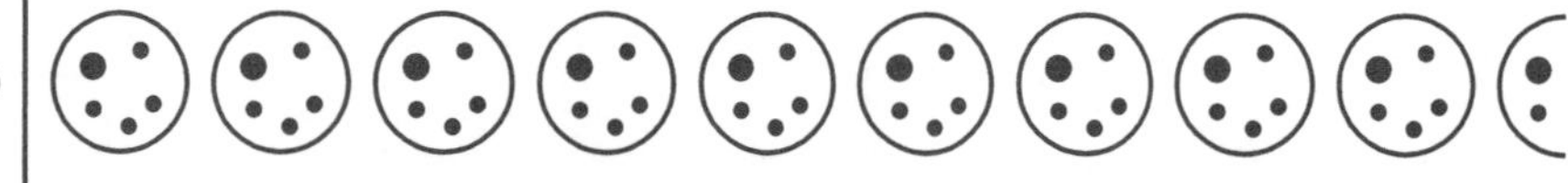

Oatmeal raisin 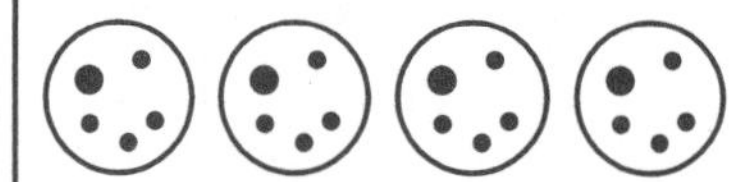

Peanut butter 

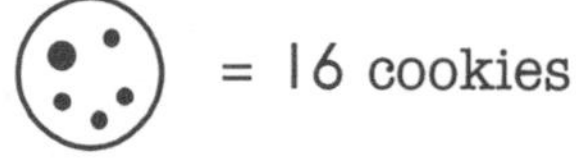 = 16 cookies



©Addison Wesley Longman, Inc./Published by Dale Seymour Publications®

**Use the facts.**

**Write a question for each answer on the Answer Sign.**

**Facts**

- Geoff jogged 3 miles each day for a week.
- Joy jogged 5 miles each day for 6 days.

---

**Complete the rules.**

**Finish the tables.**

| Multiply by ____ and add 2. | |
|---|---|
| 1 → | 5 |
| 2 | 8 |
| 3 | 11 |
| 4 | 14 |
| 5 | ____ |
| 6 | ____ |
| 10 | ____ |

| Subtract ____ and multiply by 4. | |
|---|---|
| 3 → | 8 |
| 4 | 12 |
| 5 | 16 |
| 6 | 20 |
| 7 | ____ |
| 10 | ____ |
| 21 | ____ |

| Add ____ and divide by 3. | |
|---|---|
| 1 → | 1 |
| 4 | 2 |
| 7 | 3 |
| 16 | 6 |
| 19 | 7 |
| 22 | ____ |
| 37 | ____ |



©Addison Wesley Longman, Inc./Published by Dale Seymour Publications®

**What is the start number?**

55

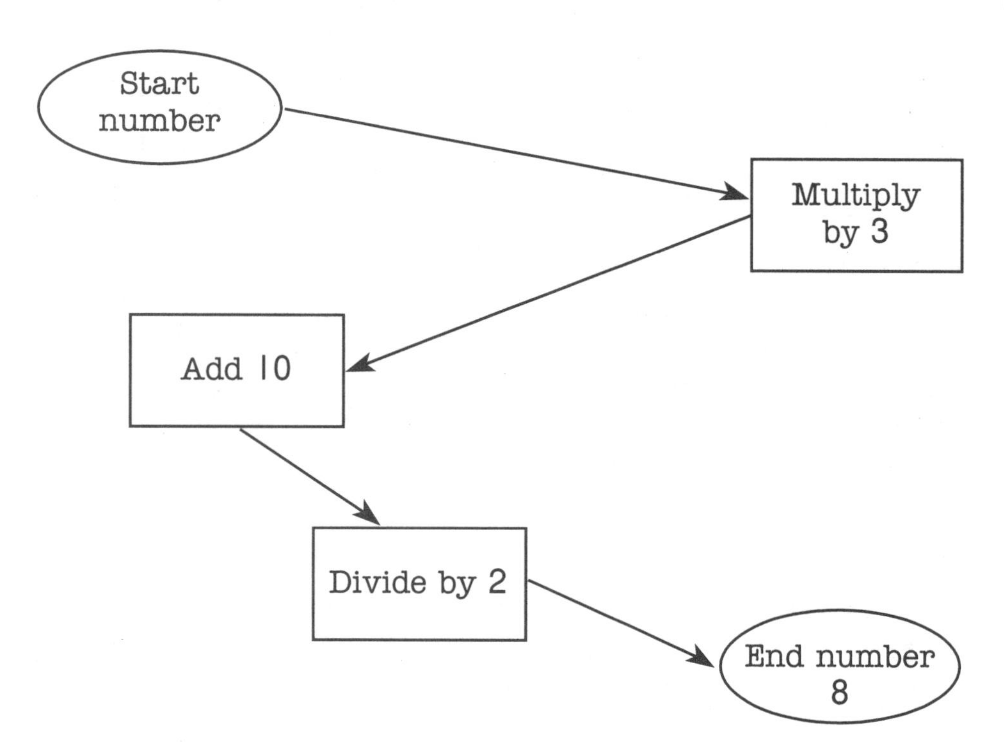


---

**Write a number in each blank.**

**The story must make sense.**

Mateo bought ______ packages of sports cards.

There are ______ cards in each package.

Mateo bought a total of ______ cards.

Mateo bought ______ more cards than Eric.

Eric bought ______ cards.

**Which numbers can you exchange in your story and still have the story make sense?**

©Addison Wesley Longman, Inc./Published by Dale Seymour Publications®

**Solve these if-then problems.**

*If*  = 30 and 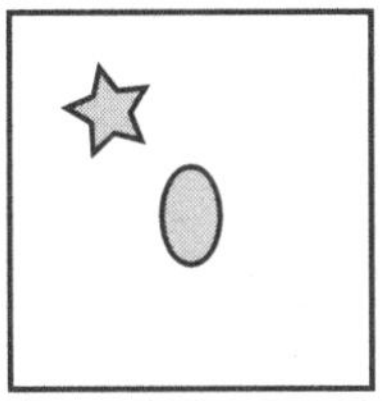 = 15 *then*  = _____

*If* 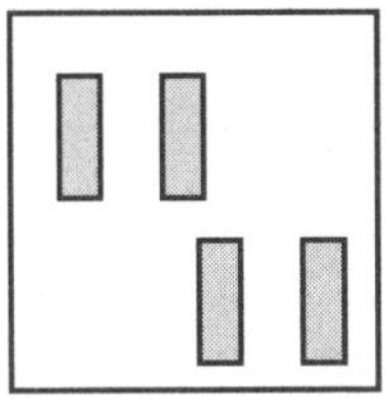 = 40 and 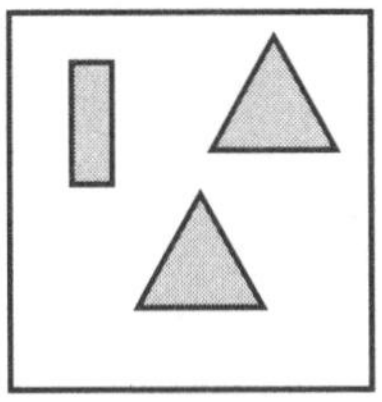 = 14 *then* 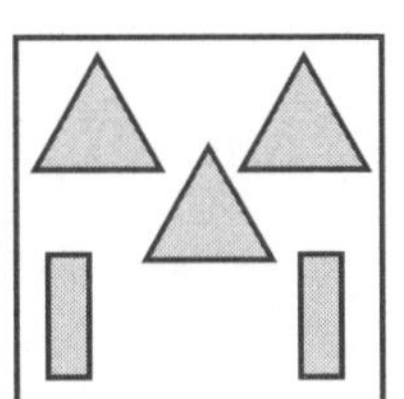 = _____

**Make up two if-then problems for a friend to solve.**



---

## Petra's Pizza Prices

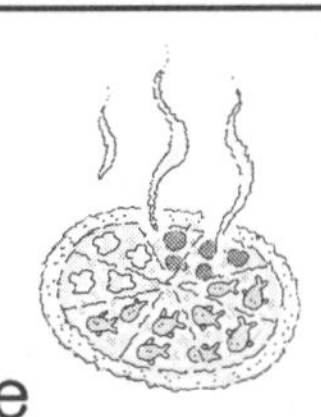

| | small | large |
|---|---|---|
| cheese | $7.50 | $8.75 |
| mushroom | $8.00 | $9.25 |
| pepperoni | $8.25 | $9.50 |
| vegetable | $8.00 | $9.25 |

**Three friends bought 2 large pepperoni pizzas to share.**

**How much should each person pay?**

©Addison Wesley Longman, Inc./Published by Dale Seymour Publications®

## 59

**The product of the three numbers on each side of this magic triangle is 72.**

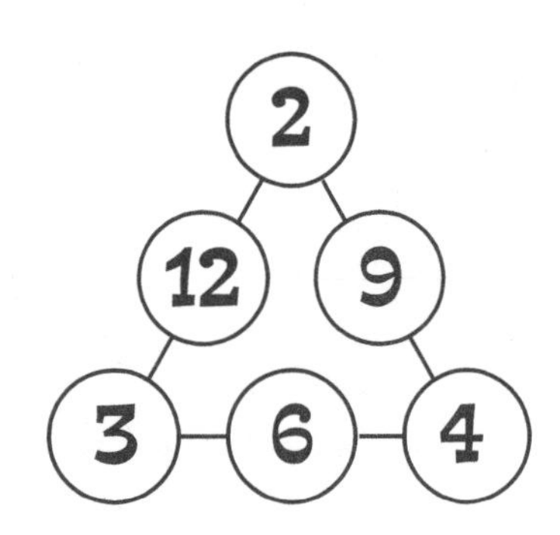


**Use the numbers shown to make another magic triangle.**

**The product of the three numbers on each side must be 60.**

3 2 10 5 4 6

---

## 60

**How many pigs are in the barn?**

**Tell how you know.**

Follow the directions on the arrows to complete the grid.

61

× 3 (arrow pointing up)

| | | | |
|---|---|---|---|
| | 36 | | |
| | 12 | 24 | |
| | | | |

(arrow pointing right) × 2



---

62

**Is the answer to 8 × 34 closer to 240 or 320?**

- 8 × 30 = 240
- 8 × 40 = 320
- 8 × 34 = ?

**Tell how you know.**

©Addison Wesley Longman, Inc./Published by Dale Seymour Publications®

**Mr. Rana has $56.**

**He wants to buy 8 T-shirts.**

**He is not sure he has enough money.**

**Tell how Mr. Rana can estimate to decide.**

---

64

**Write three story problems about the boxes of cereal.**

**Problem 1:** You must multiply to solve the problem.

**Problem 2:** You must divide to solve the problem.

**Problem 3:** You must multiply and then add to solve the problem.

## 65

# 59 190 5 7 2

**Use these numbers. Estimate to find the answers.**

- Which two numbers have a product of 118?
- Which two numbers have a quotient of 38?
- Which two numbers have a product that is greater than 11,000?
- Which two numbers have a quotient that is greater than 90?



---

## 66

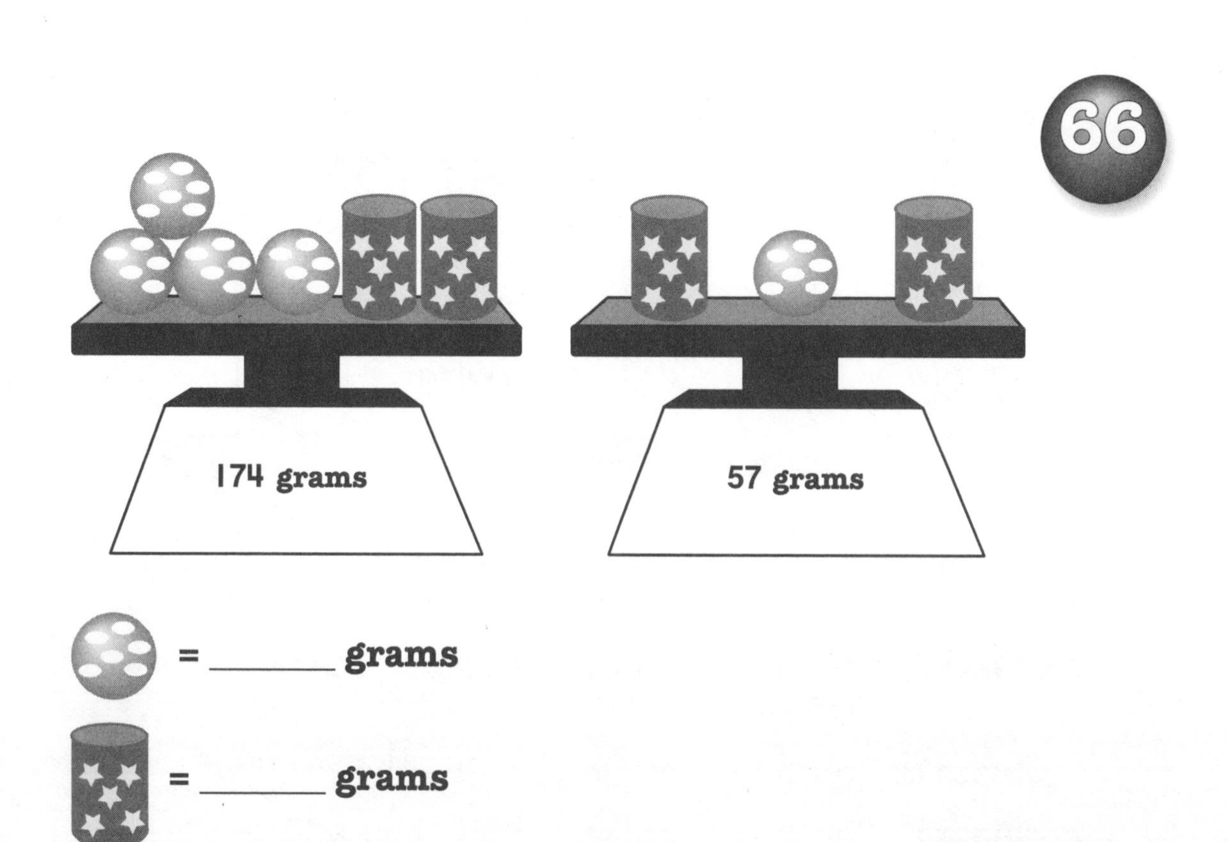

**Fill in the circles.**

**Write eight division problems in which the divisor is 5 and the remainder is 1.**

◯ ÷ 5 = ◯ R1    ◯ ÷ 5 = ◯ R1

◯ ÷ 5 = ◯ R1    ◯ ÷ 5 = ◯ R1

◯ ÷ 5 = ◯ R1    ◯ ÷ 5 = ◯ R1

◯ ÷ 5 = ◯ R1    ◯ ÷ 5 = ◯ R1

---

68

**Fill in the blanks.**

**Describe any patterns you see.**

$1 \times 3 + 1 =$ **4** $= 2 \times 2$

$2 \times 4 + 1 =$ **9** $=$ ____ $\times$ ____

$3 \times 5 + 1 =$ ____ $=$ ____ $\times$ ____

**Use your patterns to fill in these blanks.**

$5 \times 7 + 1 =$ ____ $=$ ____ $\times$ ____

$6 \times 8 + 1 =$ ____ $=$ ____ $\times$ ____

___ $\times$ ___ $+ 1 =$ ____ $= 8 \times 8$

___ $\times 14 + 1 =$ ____ $=$ ____ $\times$ ____



©Addison Wesley Longman, Inc./Published by Dale Seymour Publications®

**Circle 2 numbers in each square that have a product in the range.**

80 11 7 45 3

**Range:** 60–100

3 21 10 7 42

**Range:** 110–130

71 8 5 93 60

**Range:** 550–600

9 15 17 12 70

**Range:** 600–650

---

70

**The pattern continues.**

**What is the last number in chain 10?**

**How do you know?**

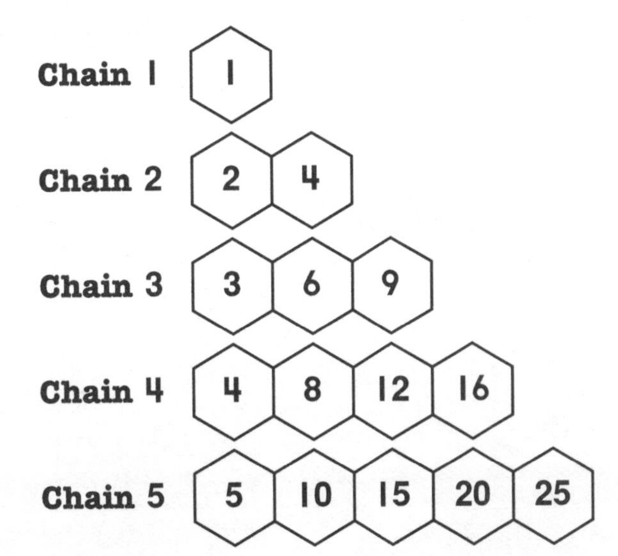


**Chain 6**

**71**

$4.25 3 $2.50
$8.25 $15.75

**Use each number shown to complete the story.**

**Your story must make sense.**

René bought _______ pairs of socks.

Each pair cost _______ .

He also bought a baseball cap for _______ .

Altogether, René spent _______ .

He gave the clerk $20. He received _______ in change.



---

**72**

**Estimate.**

**Match each shopping list with one of the totals.**

**Use a calculator to check.**

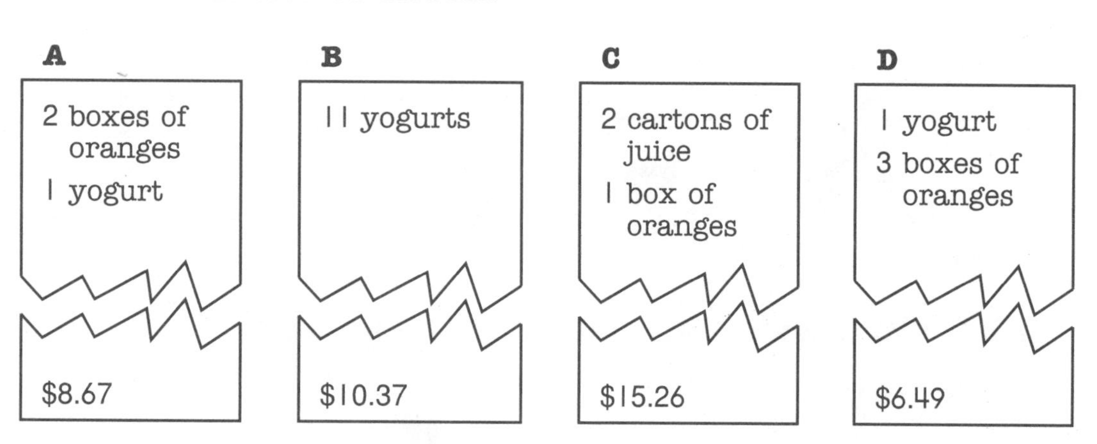

**If you know that 6 × 24 = 144, how can you find 12 × 24 without multiplying?**

---

**Fill in the boxes to get the product.**

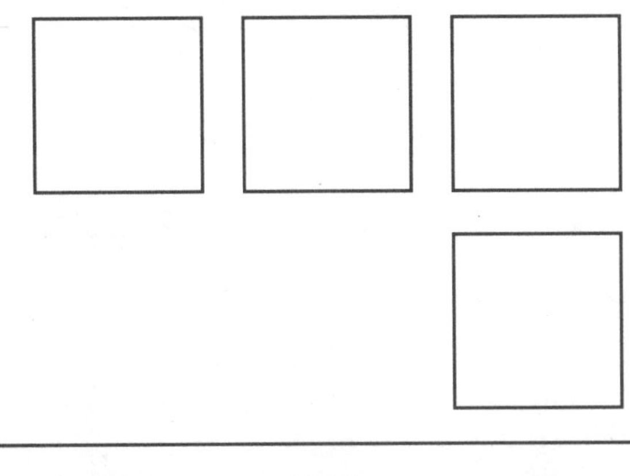

**7 2 0**

**What other ways can you fill in the boxes?**

**Record three different numbers between 0 and 10.**

| ____ | ____ | ____ |
| --- | --- | --- |
| **first** | **second** | **third** |

Multiply the first number by 5: ____

Add 35: ____

Multiply by 2: ____

Add the second number: ____

Multiply by 10: ____

Add the third number: ____

Subtract 700: ____

**Try this for two other sets of three numbers.**
**What do you notice?**

**Do you think this will always happen?**

**The Cycle Shop sells bicycles and tricycles.**

**How many bicycles are there?**

**How many tricycles are there?**

**Could there be a different answer? Explain.**

**Use your calculator.**

**Find the greatest number for** 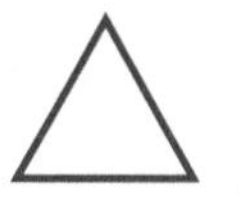 **.**

---

**You want to earn $125 to buy a bicycle.**

**What will you do?**

**How many hours will it take you to earn the money?**

©Addison Wesley Longman, Inc./Published by Dale Seymour Publications®

**Write three multiplication or division questions you can answer using the information given in the table.**

**School Data**

| Name of school | Number of teachers | Number of students |
|---|---|---|
| Baker | 25 | 620 |
| Miller | 47 | 1128 |
| King | 36 | 936 |

**Give your questions to a friend to solve.**

---

80

**Which box of crayons is the better buy?**

**How did you decide?**

Shondra bought a roll of 86 feet of ribbon.

She uses the ribbon to make bows.

She uses 1 yard of ribbon to make each bow.

How many bows can she make?

How long is the piece left over?

Tell how you found your answers.



---

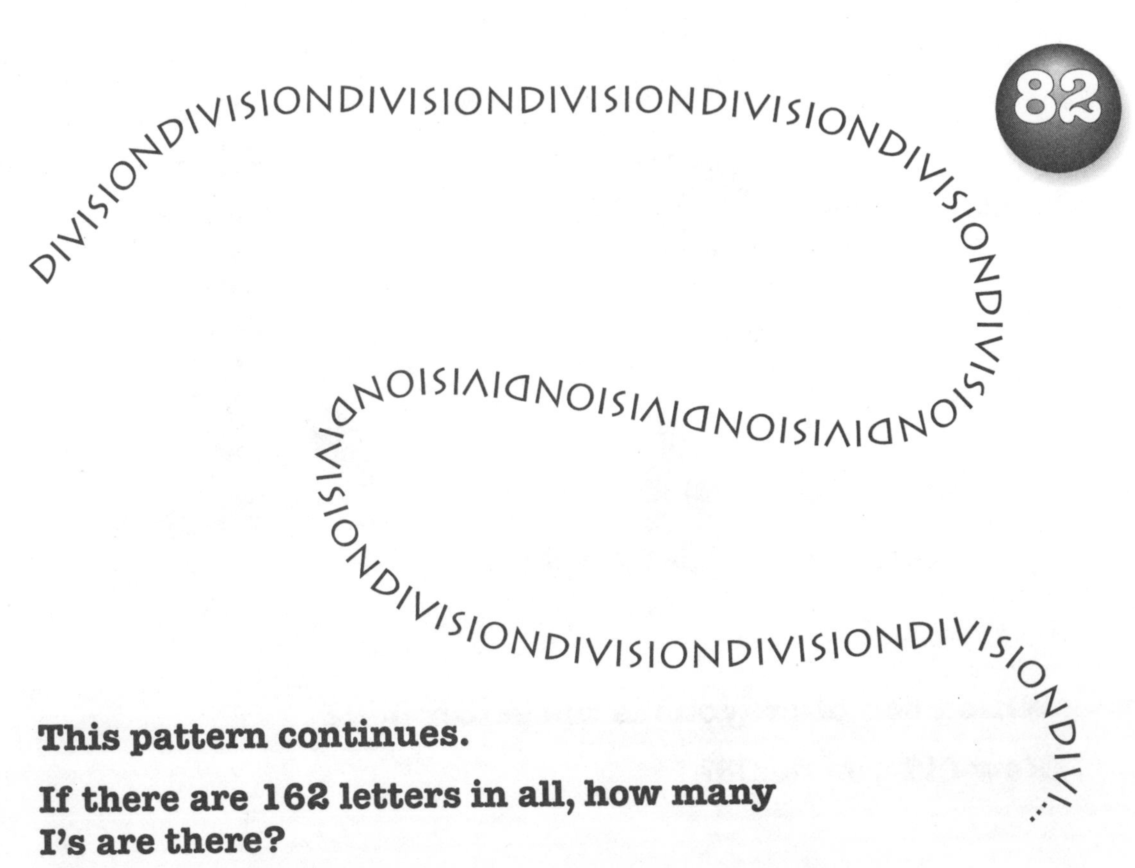


This pattern continues.

If there are 162 letters in all, how many I's are there?

83

**Clues**

- The number is between 420 ÷ 70 and 810 ÷ 90.
- The number is not equal to 560 ÷ 80.

---

**Rosa has a special way to multiply by 5.**

84

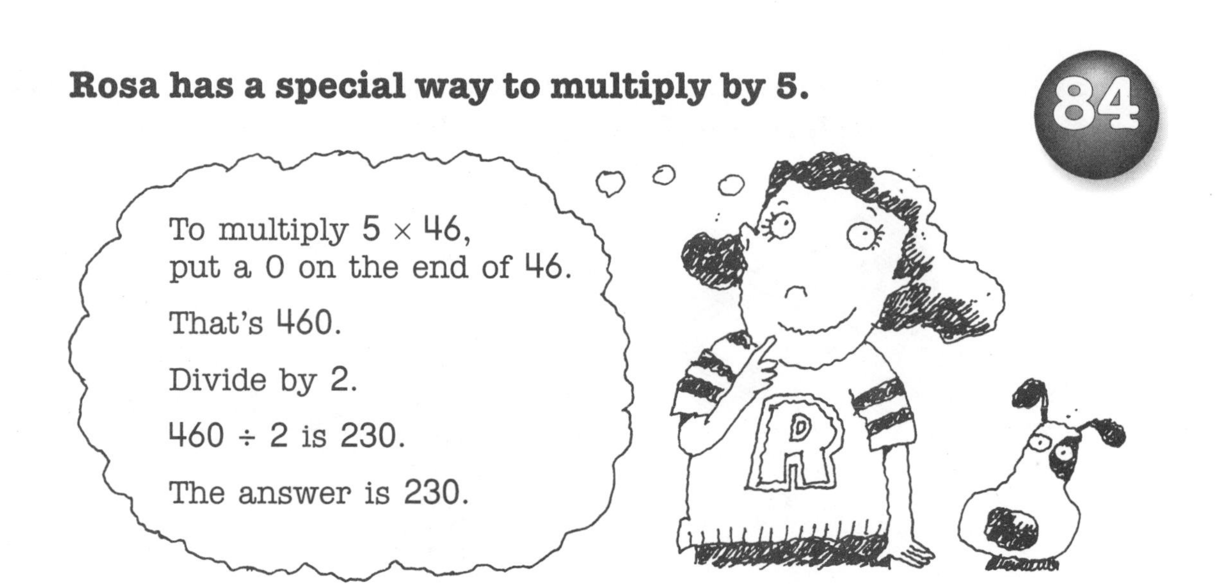


**Use Rosa's method to find these products.**

**5 × 68** **5 × 15** **5 × 57**

**Explain Rosa's method.**

# 868 2 7 198

**Choose from the given numbers to make each equation true.**

**_____ × _____ = 1386**

**_____ ÷ _____ = 99**

**_____ × _____ = 1736**

**_____ ÷ _____ = 124**

**Talk with a classmate about how you made your choices.**

**Use a calculator to check.**



---

**Suppose you want to use your calculator to find this quotient, but the [4] key is broken.**

**What can you do with your "broken" calculator to get the answer?**

**Write the steps you would follow.**

**Suppose you know that 96 ÷ 6 = 16.**

**How can you use this information to figure out 96 ÷ 12?**

---

**The Lyons family is going to a wedding in Salt Lake City, Utah.**

**The distance from their home in Atlanta, Georgia, to Salt Lake City is 1880 miles.**

**The wedding is on June 6, and the family wants to arrive one day early.**

**They plan to drive an average of 50 miles per hour, for 7 hours per day.**

**When should they begin their trip?**

**Tell how you decided.**

©Addison Wesley Longman, Inc./Published by Dale Seymour Publications®

**Jake asked 80 people which of four movies they liked best.**

**Movie Survey**

| Favorite movie | Number of people |
|---|---|
| Mary Poppins | 30 |
| Snow White | 15 |
| Peter Pan | 10 |
| The Wizard of Oz | 25 |

**Make a pictograph using Jake's data.**

**Show your legend.**

**How did you decide on the symbol to use?**

**How did you decide how many people the symbol would represent?**

**Write a different number in each empty square of the puzzle.**

**Then write a clue for each "across" and "down" number.**

**Each clue must use × or ÷.**

**Clues**

| Across | Down |
|---|---|
| 1. $24 \times 7$ | 2. |
| 3. | 4. |
| 4. | |
| 5. | |

**Use your calculator.**

**Put the same number in each □ to make the sentence true.**

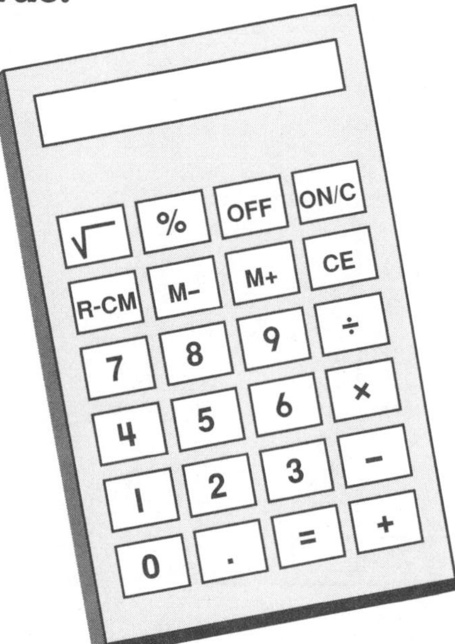


---

92

**Rosa has a special way to multiply by 9.**

To multiply 9 × 24,
put a 0 on the end of 24.

That's 240.

Subtract 24 from 240.

240 – 24 is 216.

The answer is 216.

**Use Rosa's method to find these products.**

**9 × 79** **9 × 45** **9 × 57**

**Explain Rosa's method.**

©Addison Wesley Longman, Inc./Published by Dale Seymour Publications®

**93**

**Find the missing digits.**

```
    1 [ ][ ] R [ ]
   ____________
 3 ) [ ] 7 [ ]
   - 3
   ______
     1 [ ]
   -[ ][ ]
   ______
       2 5
     -[ ][ ]
   ______
         [ ]
```

---

**94**

**Maria opened her mystery book.**

**She multiplied the numbers on the two facing pages.**

**The product was 156.**

**What were the two page numbers?**

**Solve these if-then problems.**

*If* = 24 and = 18 *then* = ____

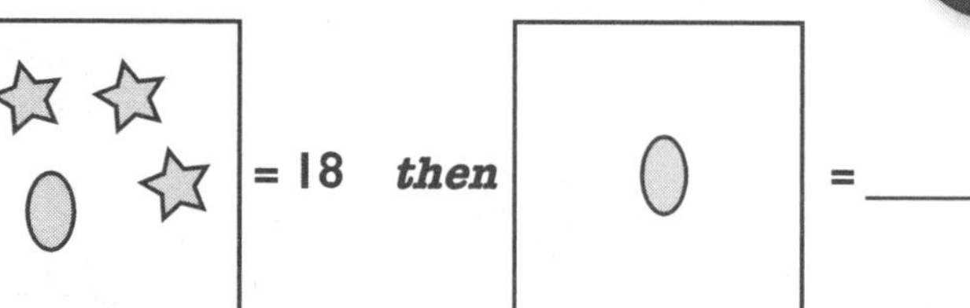

*If* = 30 and = 39 *then* = ____

**Make up two if-then problems for a friend to solve.**

---

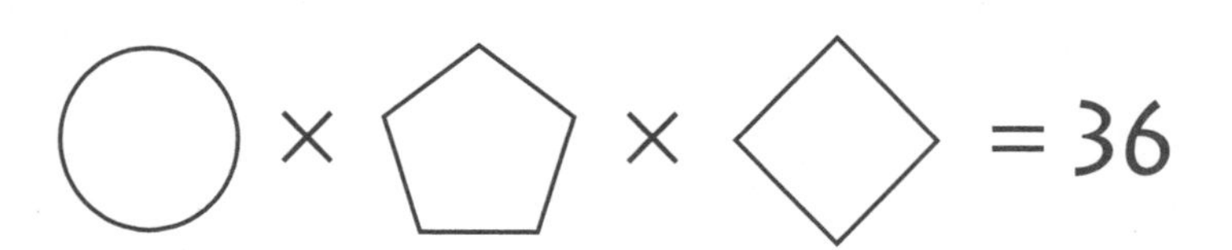

× × = 36

÷ =

>

= ____ = ____ = ____

©Addison Wesley Longman, Inc./Published by Dale Seymour Publications®

**Tell how to use a calculator to find each missing number.**

**A.** $6\overline{)\ ?\ }$ = 17R3

**B.** $?\overline{)\ 74\ }$ = 9R2

**C.** $9\overline{)115}$ = 12R?

**D.** $4\overline{)173}$ = ?R1

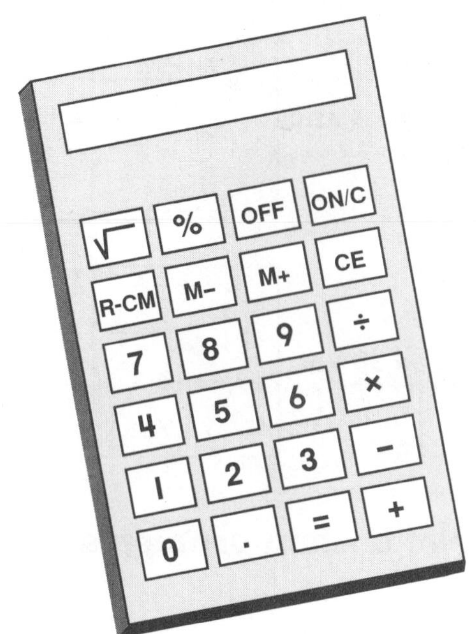


---

**What is the (carrot) doing?**

**4** (carrot) **5 = 18** **10** (carrot) **0 = 20**

**6** (carrot) **2 = 16** **24** (carrot) **6 = 60**

**Use the (carrot) rule to answer these problems:**

**6** (carrot) **0 = ____** **20** (carrot) **____ = 42**

**9** (carrot) **6 = ____** **7** (carrot) **____ = 20**

**18** (carrot) **2 = ____** **____** (carrot) **9 = 18**

99

**Use your calculator.**

**Who is correct, Maria or Leo?**

**What did you do to decide?**

---

100

$$\begin{array}{r} 87 \\ \times\ 34 \\ \hline 348 \\ 2610 \\ \hline 2958 \end{array}$$

**Use the multiplication example above to find the missing numbers.**

**87 × 30 = ______**

**87 × ______ = 34,800**

**870 × 3 = ______**

# Answers

1. 12 and 2; 12 and 3; Mysteries will vary.
2. 61
3. Alana got 12 more points than Dan.
4. Stories will vary.
5. $1.10 – $0.75 = 35¢ more in dimes
6. 16 lb; Explanations will vary.
7. Answers will vary.
8. 20 more books; Batai read 60 and Aaron read 40, so Batai read 20 more. *Or,* Batai has 2 more squares, so he read 20 more.
9. Pay for 18 tickets, get 6 tickets free.
10. 18; Original problems will vary.
11. $28
12. 4 children
13. Answers will vary.
14. 18 beads, 45 beads
15. 12 boys
16. 5 rectangles: 1 by 36, 2 by 18, 3 by 12, 4 by 9, 6 by 6
17. 12 ; Possible explanation: It takes 2 for 3 , so for 18 there are six 3s and it takes $6 \times 2 = 12$ .
18. 7 parent volunteers
19. 16 coins; Explanations will vary.
20. 5 dimes
21. 12, 24, 36, and 48; 60; Possible explanation: 12, 24, 36, and 48 are multiples of 12 (multiples of both 3 and 4), and 60 is the next multiple of 12.
22. bird stamp 15 12 9 6 3 0<br>kite stamp 0 2 4 6 8 10
23. Ben is 48. Keenan is 2.
24. 16 kg; Possible explanation: A cube is $72 \div 6 = 12$ kg, and $2 \times 12 = 24$ and $72 - 24 = 48$, so 3 spheres are 48 kg. $48 \div 3 = 16$, so there are 16 kg on scale C.
25. How much money does Paul have? (53¢) How much does Daniela have? (35¢) How much do they have in all? (88¢) How much more does Paul have than Daniela? (18¢)
26. 34 minutes; Steps will vary.
27. 6 sandwiches: tuna on wheat, white, or rye, peanut butter on wheat, white, or rye; $4 \times 5 = 20$; Explanations will vary.
28. 1 half dollar, 1 quarter, 2 dimes, 2 nickels *or* 3 quarters, 3 dimes
29. eight: 8, 12 16, 24, 32, 48, 72, 96
30. 42
31. 310 km
32. Blaire's ; Possible explanations:
    - Compare unit costs: Blaire's, $96 \div 8 = 12$¢ each; Perry's, $78 \div 6 = 13$¢ each.
    - Find the cost of 24 balloons (24 is the LCM of 6 and 8): Blaire's, $3 \times 96$¢ = $2.88; Perry's, $4 \times 78$¢ = $3.12.
33. Move 2 from C to A.
34. 48, 8, 120, 140, 20, 180, 36
35. 29 players; There are 4 basketball teams (20 players) and 1 baseball team (9 players).
36. The number of answers is infinite. Students may or may not think of using fractions, decimals, or negative numbers. Some possibilities:

| □ | 2 | 4 | 6 | 8 | 10 | 0 | 1 | 5 | –2 |
|---|---|---|---|---|---|---|---|---|---|
| △ | 9 | 8 | 7 | 6 | 5 | 10 | $9\frac{1}{2}$ | $7\frac{1}{2}$ | 11 |

37. $43 \times 5$; $87 \times 9$; The multiplier should have the greatest digit. The tens digit should be greater than the ones digit.

38. 96 petals

39. Stories will vary.

40. Answers will vary.

41. $6\overline{)34}$

42. A quarter a day for 2 weeks is \$1.95 more than a nickel a day in July.

43. \$72; Drawings will vary, but structures should have 20 blocks.

44. 4, 5, 3

45. 87¢ (7 dimes, 3 nickels, 2 pennies)

46. 364 stickers

47. Step 1: $4 \times 30 = 120$
Step 2: $4 \times 1 = 4$
Step 3: $120 - 4 = 116$
Step 4: $4 \times 29 = 116$

48. 36, 10, 6, 2, 20 or 36, 2, 6, 10, 20

49. 96¢

50. 55; Possible explanation: The last number in each level is 6 times the level number. The last number in level 9 is $6 \times 9 = 54$, so the first number in level 10 is 55.

51. 213

52. 76 cookies

53. Possible answer: How many more miles did Joy jog than Geoff? (9) How many miles did Geoff jog in all? (21) How many more miles did Joy jog than Geoff on a day they both jogged? (2) How many miles did they jog in all? (51)

54. Multiply by 3 and add 2: 17, 20, 32. Subtract 1 and multiply by 4: 24, 36, 80. Add 2 and divide by 3: 8, 13.

55. 2

56. Answers will vary; The number of packages and the number of cards in each package can always be exchanged.

57. 39; 26; Problems will vary.

58. Two friends will pay \$6.33, and one will pay \$6.34.

59. Possible triangle:

3
4 10
5 6 2

60. 8 pigs; Possible explanation: 48 legs means 12 animals, so there must be 8 pigs and 4 horses.

61.

| 54 | 108 | 216 | 432 |
|---|---|---|---|
| 18 | 36 | 72 | 144 |
| 6 | 12 | 24 | 48 |
| 2 | 4 | 8 | 16 |

62. 240; 34 is closer to 30 than 40.

63. Possible answer: Since $8 \times 7 = 56$ and the shirts are less than \$7, he has enough money.

64. Answers will vary.

65. $59 \times 2 = 118$; $190 \div 5 = 38$;
$190 \times 59 > 11{,}000$; $190 \div 2 > 90$

66. 39 grams, 9 grams

67. Answers will vary, but the dividend must be 1 more than a multiple of 5. For example: $6 \div 5 = 1$ R1, $21 \div 5 = 4$ R1, $46 \div 5 = 9$ R1.

68. Possible pattern: The first and second numbers increase by 1, the third is always 1, the fourth is a square number, and the last two are the same and are the whole number between the first two.

$2 \times 4 + 1 = 9 = 3 \times 3$

$3 \times 5 + 1 = 16 = 4 \times 4$

$5 \times 7 + 1 = 36 = 6 \times 6$

$6 \times 8 + 1 = 49 = 7 \times 7$

$7 \times 9 + 1 = 64 = 8 \times 8$

$12 \times 14 + 1 = 169 = 13 \times 13$

69. $7 \times 11, 3 \times 42, 71 \times 8, 9 \times 70$

70. 100; Possible explanation: Chain 1 is the first multiple of 1. Chain 2 is the first two multiples of 2. Chain 3 is the first three multiples of 3. Chain 10 will be the first ten multiples of 10, and $10 \times 10 = 100$.

71. 3, \$2.50, \$8.25, \$15.75, \$4.25

72. A, \$10.37; B, \$6.49; C, \$8.67; D, \$15.26

73. Add the answer to $6 \times 24$ to itself: $144 + 144 = 288$.

74. 6 ways: $720 \times 1, 360 \times 2, 240 \times 3, 180 \times 4, 144 \times 5$, and $120 \times 6$

75. The hundreds, tens, and ones digits are the first, second, and third numbers, respectively. Noting that this happens in 3 cases, students will likely answer yes, though some may have doubts.

76. The number of answers is infinite. For example: 6 bicycles and 4 tricycles or 12 bicycles and 8 tricycles.

77. 383 is the greatest whole number.

78. Answers will vary.

79. Questions will vary.

80. 12 for \$1.50; Possible explanation: 12 crayons at the 6-crayon price would be $2 \times 0.99 = \$1.98$, which is more than \$1.50.

81. 28 bows, 2 feet; Explanations will vary.

82. 61

83. 8

84. The products are $680 \div 2 = 340$, $150 \div 2 = 75$, and $570 \div 2 = 285$. To multiply by 5, Rosa first multiplies by 10 and then divides by 2.

85. $198 \times 7 = 1386$; $198 \div 2 = 99$; $868 \times 2 = 1736$; $868 \div 7 = 124$

86. Possible answer: Divide 632 by 8 to get 79 and then multiply by 2 to get 158. Thus $632 \div 4 = 158$.

87. Since 12 is twice 6, the quotient will be half of $96 \div 6$, or half of 16, or 8.

88. May 31; Possible explanation: At 350 miles per day, they will arrive on the sixth day of travel.

89. Answers will vary.

90. Answers will vary.

91. $25 \times 25 = 625$

92. $790 - 79 = 711$; $450 - 45 = 405$; $570 - 57 = 513$; To multiply by 9, Rosa thinks of 9 as $10 - 1$.

93.
```
   1 5 8 R 1
3)4 7 5
 -3
  1 7
 -1 5
    2 5
   -2 4
       1
```

94. 12 and 13

95. 3; 8

96. 3, 2, 6

97. A, 105; Multiply 17 and 6, add 3 to the product. B, 8; Subtract 2 from 74, divide the difference by 9 *or* divide 74 by 9 and ignore the decimal. C, 7; Multiply 12 and 9 and subtract the product from 115. D, 43; Subtract 1 from 173 and divide the difference by 4.

98. The carrot is multiplying each number by 2 and then adding the products. *Or,* the carrot adds the two numbers and multiplies the sum by 2. From left to right: 12, 1, 30, 3, 40, 0

99. Maria is correct because 4,993,200 minutes is about 9.5 years: $4{,}993{,}200 \div 60 \div 24 \div 365 = 9.5$.

100. 2610; 400; 2610